THE ALTRUIST

The Untold Story of Dookhee Gungah in Twentieth Century Mauritius

Swetam Gungah

H
HANSIB

Published in Great Britain by Hansib Publications in 2023

Hansib Publications Limited
76 High Street, Hertford, SG14 3TA, UK

info@hansibpublications.com
www.hansibpublications.com

ISBN 978-1-7395636-0-8
ISBN 978-1-7395636-1-5 (Kindle)
ISBN 978-1-7395636-2-2 (ePub)

A CIP catalogue record for this book
is available from the British Library

Design & Production by Hansib Publications Ltd
Printed in Great Britain

To my father

Dookhee Gungah – his life and achievements

Contents

Fowdur, my great-great-grandfather sets sail from his native India to Mauritius in 1854, and thus begins the story

Fowdur's sons, including Dookhee and my great-grandfather Raghubur, establish a rich legacy

Raghubur's son, Khemraj, safeguards the religious and cultural legacy in the early 20th century

Khemraj's son, Kooshalanund, initiates the research about the family history, and keeps the memory alive with the Dookhee Gungah school and Khemraj Gungah preschool

Kooshalanund, my father, is my inspiration. And my aspiration is to carry on his work, and share Dookhee's story with the world

Preface

When I was at school, an atlas was a textbook from which every child had to memorise the names of all the rivers, mountains and sugar mills of Mauritius. It had everything you needed to know about Mauritian geography. On the other hand, we didn't have a textbook that taught us Mauritian history in as much detail. In fact, some important bits were left out. We were taught that when slavery was abolished in Mauritius in 1834, labourers were brought from India to replace the enslaved Africans who had worked on the sugar plantations; and then, lo and behold, Mauritius finally gained her independence in 1968 from the British. It all seemed too straightforward; too easy; too uneventful; but none of us young minds thought to question this narrative any further. Most people, I would wager, still don't know much about this episode of the British Empire when, much before the partition of India and Pakistan, there was a mass migration of Indians. This is not something we can simply glance over. It has left its indelible footprint on the world, and it cannot remain a footnote in our history books.

The British needed a new form of labour to replace the enslaved Africans in 1834 and chose Mauritius, from among their several other colonies, to be the sandbox for what it called the Great Experiment where labourers from India would be brought to work on the plantations on a fixed-term contract. They had to ensure that this new system would be economically worthwhile before they could deploy it across the Empire. The first attempt at importing Indian labourers in 1829 had failed so they needed this one to work given that time was running out to find a substitute workforce. Fortunately for the British, it did. And as a result, two million Indians were sent across the globe as part of the indentureship.

Over a perilous and fateful journey that lasted weeks, the ship, *Atlas*, carried in her belly thirty-six Indians destined to work in the sugarcane fields on a distant island. And so was born the modern indentured labour diaspora on 2nd November 1834, as the recruits arrived in Mauritius to start a new life. These immigrants would leave their footprints not just on this one shore but, metaphorically, across several other countries within the realm of the British Empire due to the favourable outcome of the experiment. Favourable for some, I should emphasise.

During my most recent visit to Mauritius in 2023, I purchased a model of the *Atlas*. This ship holds a sentimental value for me. The first member of my family to arrive in Mauritius came on board a ship called the *Prince Albert* in 1854. But it was thanks to the successful voyage of the *Atlas* that a fleet of other ships eventually brought nearly half a million Indians to Mauritius, my great-great-grandfather included. Not every descendant of the Indian immigrants who had settled in Mauritius chooses to reconnect with their past. For some, there is a deep sense of shame associated with the memory of indentureship. For others, this is a thing of the past and not worth dwelling on. For me, it has been a journey of discovery. And the more I peered into my past, the more it became clear to me that what matters most is our future. And our future is defined by our legacy.

What we leave behind is worth more than what we take from this world, if what we leave behind is something good, something that has bettered the lives of others. Whoever we are, whatever our background, however brief our time has been on this planet, we each leave a memory, a feeling, a legacy behind. And there are those whose legacy is a garden where the happiness of others can bloom. One such individual is an ancestor of mine. I am extremely fortunate to be able to trace my lineage back to a person who has had an enormous influence on his community and his fellow compatriots.

I have always admired the greats such as Einstein and Beethoven. Then, of course, like so many children, I have emulated the superheroes and the silver screen idols in whom I was in awe. I did not lack much in terms of characters and personalities, fictional or otherwise, who would enthuse me. But then, until about a decade ago, when I delved deeper into the life of my great-grandfather, I gradually came to realise that I needn't look any further, anymore. I finally found that person, that hero, who I had always been seeking as a true inspiration. It is said that the thing you were most in need of has always been right there staring back at you this whole time, but you simply weren't looking. In fact, you were searching everywhere else except inside you. And in my case, that which I was seeking the most is literally in me, in my genes, and this realisation fills me with a deep sense of humility.

I have spent years trying to understand the life of my great-grandfather, Dookhee Gungah. He had passed away long before I was born, so the only knowledge I have of him comes mostly from my father, my immediate relatives and a few historians who have written about him. But until recently I could not grasp the real essence of who he was beyond the stories, though very detailed and inspirational, that have been told about him.

I had to look underneath the surface, the superficial, and peel layers after layers to form a more solid, three-dimensional picture of that person. And during that long process, several questions raised their heads and, with intriguing eyes, gazed at me. I had no choice but to address them with due respect and figure out through whose lens was I peering at history.

What I mean is that it didn't suffice to answer each question directly, but I had to probe them further until I seized their true intention. All these questions were ultimately pushing me to challenge notions such as *identity*, *aetiology* and *servitude*.

I do not want to go into an academic deconstruction of what identity means; but identity is something we feel we know what it stands for even if we don't have the full vocabulary to explain it. We know who we are. Yet, for me, identity is not static. It has changed from something tied to a broader concept, like nationality, to something linked to my ancestral, as opposed to native, origin. I have wrestled with this concept for years and even though I am able to resolve this more and more (much like bringing a blurred image gradually into focus), I am not certain if behind it is one single notion. It could very well be several notions that, when brought together, give rise to our sense of identity. I don't know if I will ever find the answer to this and bring this search to a conclusion.

One conclusion that I have reached, following these long quests and intellectual meanderings, is that my great-grandfather was philanthropy personified. Put simply, he embodied the real essence of compassion and love of humanity.

Although I could fashion a better image of him, by examining his achievements, it was not the complete picture. As an individual, not only are we defined by our character, our personality, our thoughts and actions, but also by our surroundings, the environment around us, our community, our society, our norms and beliefs. The context within which we live also forms us as a person. And so, we have to consider what a person is relative to the circumstances surrounding their being. A candle in the dark, gloomy night is worth more than a torch in broad daylight.

The other point which stood out during my research was that the issues my ancestor dealt with and, in many cases, pioneered, were timeless and fundamental. Today, things like entrepreneurship, emancipation, leadership, social revolution and philanthropy are topical, even mundane to an extent, given how often these are cited by so many. Yet, given the context within which my great-grandfather lived, to be a champion of these different qualities was far from trivial.

The world into which Dookhee Gungah was born was not the most welcoming. In 1866, there was an outbreak of malaria, then an unknown disease on the island. Insufficient amounts of quinine to deal with it and the tropical climate – conducive to the proliferation of mosquitoes – meant that the epidemic lasted far longer than anyone would have anticipated. The mortality rate hit its peak in 1867, the year Dookhee was born. In total, over three years, the disease wiped out a ninth of the total population. The desolation that ensued was utterly soul-wrenching.

Before the disease struck, music filled the air as the merry piano melodies would echo in every street of the capital city, Port Louis. There was a busyness and gaiety that kept the heart of the country beating. But then came the disease, and the song and laughter ceased. The only word that was in every thought and on every lip was *fever*. Joyfulness faded like a sunset, and mourning engulfed the hearts of the citizens. Soon, the entire island fell victim to this atrocious ailment as relays of men kept digging, night and day, grave after grave. And as though one calamity was not enough, the following year, in 1868, a violent cyclone caused such immense devastation that it took years to rebuild the basic infrastructures.

This was the dismal world in which Dookhee was born but managed to survive. Here, already, were the signs that, come what may, he would endeavour to overcome the obstacles, and albeit with his family's support.

Throughout his life there would be much adversity, whether from cyclones, particularly the most notorious one in

1892; or torrential floods; or the bubonic plague of 1899 that kept reappearing until 1917; or whether from diseases introduced from abroad in 1901 that would decimate cattle and other livestock; or riots breaking out all over the island in 1911; while in the sugar plantations a disease would destroy most of the crops and therefore the livelihoods of the estate owners. Despite these many setbacks, Dookhee rose to be a beacon who would light the paths of the downtrodden.

* * * * *

This book is in two parts. Part One is a short biography of my ancestor, Dookhee Gungah. I hope it will provide a glimpse of the person he was and the impact he had on the people, the social norms and the events around him. Out of the several lessons we could learn from him, there is one which sticks with me the most: be kind, for out of kindness springs holiness.

Part Two focuses on the book, *History of Mauritius* by Pandit Atmaram Vishwanath. This part of the book provides further context to the narrative in Part One. Vishwanath was a scholar and journalist who was also a close collaborator of Dookhee Gungah during the latter part of his life. These two men were immensely significant in the popularisation of the Hindi language and culture, and the dissemination of free education in Mauritius. There have been reprints of the book ever since its first publication in 1923. However, it seemed appropriate to me to commemorate its centenary while appreciating the significance of such a book in Mauritius.

This may seem like a mere fragment of history that might easily be glanced over or even forgotten, but its importance is undeniable. The contribution by Dookhee Gungah and Pandit Atmaram Vishwanath to literacy and to the emancipation of society cannot be underestimated. Besides, there is nothing more unselfish than the spread of knowledge.

PART ONE

The Legend of Dookhee Gungah

"Absence is to love, what wind is to fire.
It extinguishes the small but kindles the great."

ROGER DE BUSSY-RABUTIN

New Shores – 1850s to 1890s

Was born to Busmoteea a boy, in the bleak of night

I t had been two weeks since she gave birth, and her body was still shattered from the pain of childbirth. She was barely sixteen. It was not uncommon for girls her age to become mothers. Or even widows. An unprecedented outbreak of malaria in December 1866 caused havoc, and forty thousand lives, or 12 per cent of the population, had perished due to this epidemic. The living conditions, in ordinary times, were already grim for Busmoteea and other indentured labourers working on the sugarcane plantations; the surge in deaths in 1867 brought even more gloom. And so, when Busmoteea and her husband, Fowdur, welcomed their first-born, they named him *Dookhee*, a Hindi word epitomising this general state of anxiety and grief[1]. That the wheel of fortune would turn for them, by the end of the 1800s, was beyond their wildest of dreams.

Fowdur's dream was to seek a better life for his family. In late August 1854, he took a fateful decision to leave the barren fields of his native village, Ruwanee, in the impoverished district of Arrah, in Bihar, to travel to Kolkata, some three hundred miles away. Whilst boarding the *Prince Albert*, he,

---

1. Over the few years preceding Dookhee's birth, the country was struck by cholera outbreaks in 1854, 1856 and 1859, devastating lives and livelihoods. Severe flooding in 1865 was a blow to the sugarcane industry, particularly in the north of the island. This was followed by drought, further affecting sugar production. Meanwhile, floods in northern India prompted more Indians to flee to Mauritius. As a result, the sugar estates and villages were overcrowded, exacerbating the spread of diseases. An unprecedented social and economic crisis ensued as several estates and planters went broke. The sense of despair and grief was palpable and seemed insurmountable. Amidst this desolation was born Dookhee.

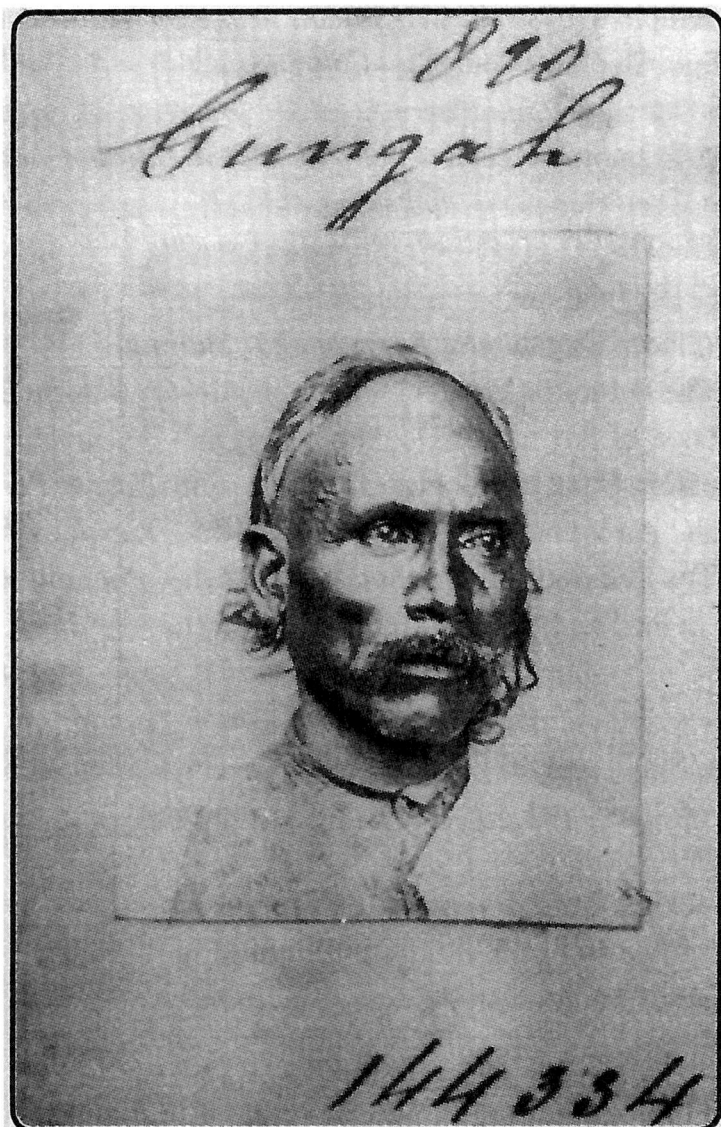

Fowdur Gungah - immigrant 144334

like hundreds of others on the ship, had no idea where he was heading to, except to a distant land of promised treasures. Most of them, if not all of them, had never even seen the sea until that day. They came unprepared – all they wanted was to flee the misery at any cost. To sail these waters was more than a leap of faith into the darkness. It meant letting go of all their possessions, material and otherwise. It meant leaving behind their family, their loved ones, and their people. It meant, more than anything, shedding that taut cast they were born with: their caste. By embarking on this journey, they were to be reborn – unless they perished crossing the Kala Paani[2]. On the other side of the ocean, that faraway land was no paradise; cholera had only just dwindled away, resulting in the death of eight thousand souls, over a period of four months.

* * * * *

Fowdur finally disembarked in Port Louis, Mauritius, along with the other young and abled men, and was taken to the nearby coolie depot on the 27th of September 1854. The officials requested his surname, to which he replied: "Gungah", formally registering as an indentured labourer. Was it his father's name that he had taken as his family name, or was he alluding to Ganga, the river on whose once fertile banks he grew up? Thus began the new life of this immigrant, then only twenty-five years old, on this exotic little island in the Indian Ocean, thousands of miles from his drought and famine-stricken village. But his journey was not quite over. From the depot, he was then sent to the sugar estate in Deux Bras, on the south-eastern part of the island. He never imagined that he

---

2. The indentured labourers expressed their fears of crossing the Kala Paani, literally the Black Water. According to Hinduism, crossing the seas would cause the loss of social respectability, and the ordinary folk were terrified of this prospect. Eventually, the British took water from the Ganges in large containers on board the ships, to reassure the Indians and protect the sanctity of life with the possibility of reincarnation beyond the sea.

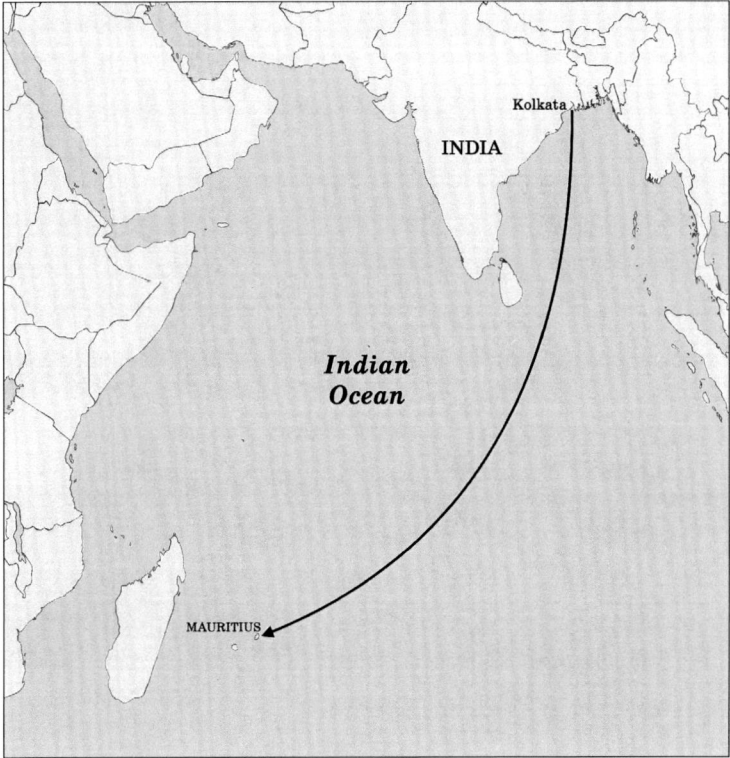

Voyage to Mauritius

would not see his family ever again and was on his own despite being surrounded by his peers, his *jahaji bhaiyon*[3].

Busmoteea was too young to understand why she and her family had undertaken a similar journey from their village in the district of Ballia, Bihar, to Kolkata and then, eventually, to Mauritius. And she certainly could not conceive how her parents, and thousands of other immigrants before them, had been duped by unscrupulous profiteers and purveyors of dreams when they were enrolled as indentured labourers. The nightmare began as soon as they boarded the ship. Traversing

---

3. Jahaji bhai (*plural*: jahaji bhaiyon) literally means boat brother. It refers to the term the Indians who undertook the same perilous journey called each other as they felt bound by the same hardship and suffering.

the Indian Ocean must have felt like an eternity. The conditions on board were cramped; deplorable to say the least. The men were separated from the women and children. They were all kept in the lower decks, sharing the same unsanitary space as the rodents. The spread of diseases was inevitable and those who were sick beyond any hope were left to die with no dignity, their bodies tossed overboard, like empty husks.

Those who were fortunate enough to set foot upon Mauritius were swiftly assigned to their respective sugar estates, to begin a life of toil and hardship. Busmoteea, this frail, innocent six-year-old child, disembarked from the *Devonshire*, on the 28th of July 1857[4] and was taken to the Deux Bras sugar estate a few days later. In all probability, as a little girl, she was groomed to be a good housewife as she helped with the domestic chores rather than being sent to work in the fields. The fact that Fowdur came to ask Busmoteea in marriage nearly a decade later implies that both he and Busmoteea's family had taken the decision to not return to India at the end of their five-year servitude[5]. Perhaps the prospect of a better life in Mauritius seemed more of a reality than ever before. They must have heard from each incoming batch of new immigrants how rough and rotten things still were in Bihar for them to forego their return journey, which they had to pay for themselves. Or was it the thought of

---

4. Meanwhile, the siege of Arrah was taking place in India. It lasted from the 27th of July to the 3rd of August during the Indian Rebellion of 1857. The rebellion had begun in May near Delhi that year and spread to other parts of northern India, including Arrah. It is estimated that at least 800 000 Indians were killed due to the rebellion and the famines and epidemics of disease that it caused in those areas. Had Busmoteea and her family not left their village, they likely would have fallen victim to the rebellion or famine.

5. The indenture agreement set out the terms and conditions under which the labourers were to be taken to the different colonies. One of the conditions was that the period of service was five years from the date of arrival in the colony. At the end of that period, the labourer may choose to return to India at their own expense. Often, the words *girmit* and *girmityas* are associated with the Indian indentured labourers. Etymologically speaking, *girmit* is the Indian pronunciation of "agreement", the contract that bound those immigrants to a life of servitude, albeit temporary.

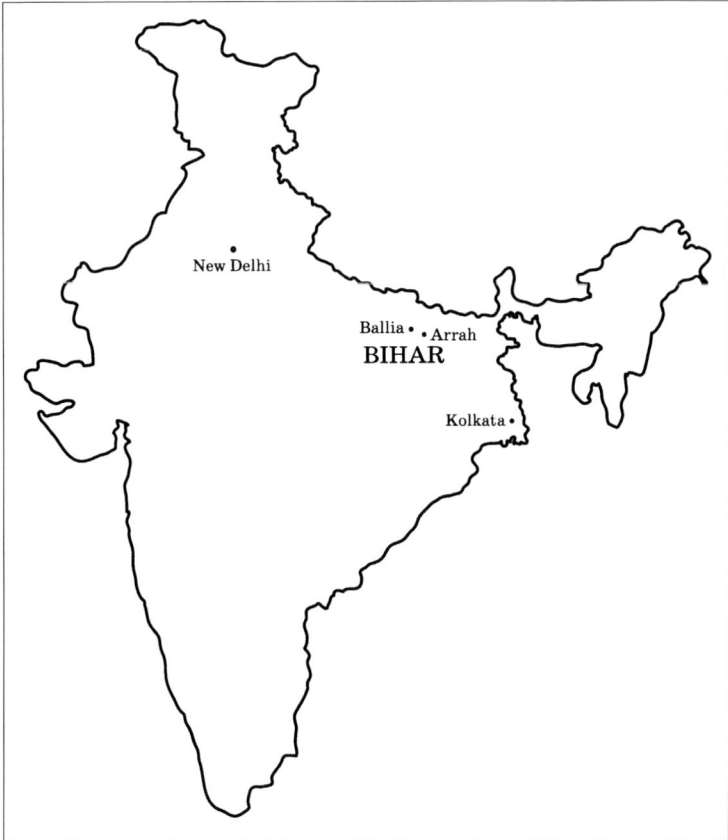

India

crossing the perilous ocean, once more, that had put them off?
The following year, in 1867, in a tattered thatched hut nestled
in the Deux Bras sugar estate, Busmoteea gave birth to
Dookhee Gungah, on the 11th day of a cold and biting August.
Fowdur, wrought with anticipation, was filled with joy to see
his wife cuddle their new-born son.

Slavery Abolished Across the British Empire

B ritish administrators in Mauritius took three months to transition from slavery to indentured servitude when the first wave of Indian immigrants[6] reached Port Louis, the capital city, on the 2nd of November 1834. However, it was not until a further three months that the abolition of slavery was officially recognised, on the 1st of February 1835. To fill the void created by the gradual retreat of slaves from the sugar plantations, Indian indentured labourers were brought over. That was known as 'The Great Experiment'. The British had to validate whether this new form of labour would prove economically viable, and socially acceptable, before it was deployed across the rest of the Empire. The experiment seemed to have worked. A total of more than one million Indians were shipped across the globe between 1834 and 1924, of which more than four-hundred and fifty thousand were taken to Mauritius alone.

The Indians landed at what is now called the *Aapravasi Ghat*, an immigration depot located in the harbour of Port Louis. They came with barely anything: their belly filled with nothing but apprehension, their heart bursting with hope and their mind full of aspiration. What they did bring was their courage, and their most precious possessions, their holy books; the *Bhagavad Gita* and the *Ramayana* were what anchored

---

6. There were contracted workers from India who were brought to Mauritius during the French rule (1710-1810) and when the British took over in 1810, but they were not part of the indentureship system that was formally institutionalised in 1834.

them to their motherland, upon setting foot in Mauritius. Their sacred scriptures offered solace and strength, in the face of brutal reality and hardships. Most never gave up their religion despite the challenges encountered. While some Indians were coerced into converting to Christianity, the religion of the colonial landlords and estate owners, others felt starved of their cultural identity and stripped of their foreparents' heritage. Their sense of 'self' and 'community' seemed to gradually disappear. As the number of Indian immigrants grew, over the decades, prayer ceremonies became more of a social gathering. Not solely religious in function, these also served as a social device to maintain community cohesion, providing hope and comfort.

Initially, there were barely any temples or socio-cultural institutions which could benefit the community, and the few who built shrines for their deities did an invaluable service to society. Indeed, the year Dookhee was born, one of the first Hindu temples was established in a village, in the north of the island by a landowner named Gokul. Even then, holding ceremonies and rituals (called puja) proved quite a mission as the items and ingredients to be used as offerings during the prayers were not readily available. Besides conducting prayers and social gatherings, they also needed a way to disseminate religious teachings. Steadily, as the Indo-Mauritian community organised itself in their individual groups, these places of learning and enlightenment, known as a baitka, saw the light of day and, in turn, cemented the community, bolstering their sense of belonging. Although a number of indentured labourers chose to return to India at the end of their five-year contract, the vast majority of those who came to Mauritius decided to call it home, as community spirit strengthened. Even though these baitkas served a valuable purpose, by the time Dookhee was of school age, in 1873, he was part of the 98 per cent of the forty thousand children aged between five and fourteen who did not receive any formal education. It was as if one had to choose either to wield a cutlass in a sugarcane field or to write in a copybook in a classroom. Such was their fate. Four decades had elapsed since the new labour system replaced slavery; nevertheless, the working conditions were still deplorable in the 1870s. Labourers were powerless, the police corrupt and violent, magistrates, ignorant and partial. Already poorly remunerated and heavily taxed, the labourers had to pay for any license to carry out an occupation. In addition, the then Governor of the island, Arthur Gordon, believed that the conditions were so dire that he deemed them to be beyond improvement. The entire country was indebted; the soil in the coastal regions was poor and not conducive to

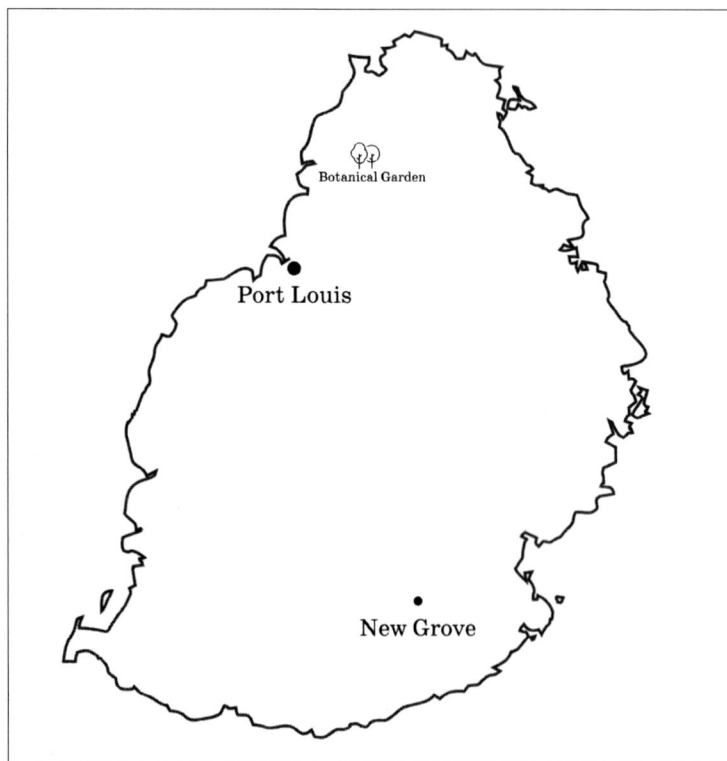

Botanical Garden

Port Louis

New Grove

Mauritius

the cultivation of sugarcane. Even worse, malaria had made a comeback.

This was Dookhee's childhood. By 1880, now a teenager and the eldest of five boys, he was expected to work the fields alongside his father, to help with the household income. An extra pair of hands meant extra savings, as well as expenditures, with the arrival of new siblings. Their spirit of unity as a family was vital to their emancipation. Their resolve paid off, but they had to be thrifty about their lifestyle. Mirroring Fowdur's sense of sacrifice, the boys worked additional hours, starting much before dawn. The Gungah brothers were not only renowned for their physical prowess but also their unwavering perseverance. Within a decade, the family had managed to buy a larger plot of land in the neighbouring village of New Grove, built themselves a better house, and could finally afford a more decent standard of living.

In 1892, Fowdur, now sixty-three, became a father for the eighth time. Once again, it was a boy! Dookhee was twenty-five then and he gradually took on the role of the head of the family, ensuring that his parents and siblings lived in comfort, exempt from a meagre income, a basic staple of rice and dal, and arduous physical work – the norm of the day.

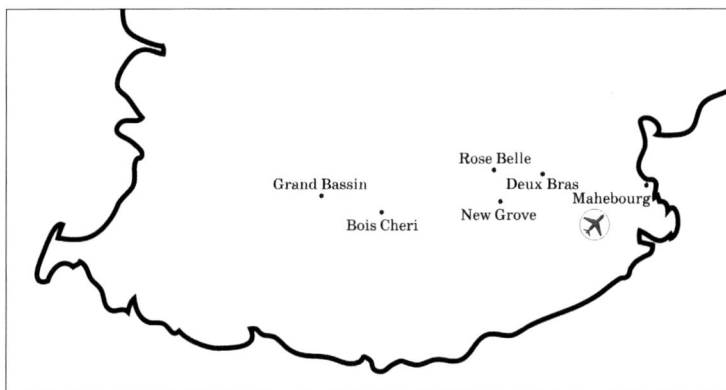

Southern Mauritius

That year, the prospects seemed most favourable for sugarcane planters; they had fought against low prices of sugar and beetroot competition on the international market, and weathered the relatively mild cyclone season in February. Everything was set to welcome a new era of prosperity for the country. Even the British administrators, eighty years after having taken over the running of the country from the French, considered the island to be the most beautiful and fertile landscape of the colony, at least in the Eastern hemisphere. In particular, in the north of the island, the Botanical Garden in Pamplemousses, which was then the third of its kind in the world, was resplendent with lush flora and luxuriant display of tropical vegetation. In all aspects, Mauritius was a pearl in the ocean.

Tragically, a cyclone of such devastating fury hit Mauritius on the 29th of April that, by the time the sun had set that day, *"the island had lost its beauty, the cane its promise, the planters their hopes, and the gardens their charms."* This sad recount was what the Lieutenant-Governor, Mr H Jerningham, had reported later that evening. He continued, *"1100 people were killed, 2000 wounded, 50 thousand left homeless; the spoilt canes of sugar laid flat upon the soil with their gone leaves revealing how full of sugar they were; sugar-mills were wrecked, crushing men women children who had sought refuge under their solid walls; Port Louis was levelled to the ground, every Indian hut blown away, whole villages swept away; trees that were more than a century old and 3 metres wide were felled to the ground, huge stone columns collapsed like a pack of cards..."* Nature, it seemed, had dealt Mauritius a bad hand. Fortunately, the Gungah family made it through this calamity, and plodded on, but not without coming to the help of those in need. Their sense of compassion and concern for their community were qualities they valued, for they, too, were once at the mercy of these vagaries.

Two years later, the price of sugar had fallen globally. For the labourers, this meant low income in order to compensate for plantation losses; the result being – longer working hours for similar wages. Some knew how to capitalise on that downturn, making both fortuitous and wise investments by purchasing plantations, large and small, that were running at a loss. Dookhee seized this opportunity, acquiring his first major plot of land of twenty arpents (approximately twenty acres). This would mark the beginning of Dookhee's golden age, an enterprise that would vastly change the lives of the Gungah family.

The Golden Years – 1900s to 1930s

By the turn of the century (1900), the migration of Indians to Mauritius had spanned over six decades. Still, only a few small temples had been established on the island, except for a rather magnificent one in the village of Triolet in the north. It was built in 1895 by Sanjibandlall Ramsoondur who, like others, recognised that the lack of temples inherently led to the inability of immigrants to maintain their religious identity. And this strong sense of religious identity was vital for community cohesion. Around that time, a sadhu named Gaurdas, of Bengali origin, travelled the island requesting assistance to build a temple. It wasn't until he reached New Grove that he received significant and unconditional help, both financially and otherwise, from Dookhee. A village, called Rose Belle, not far from where Dookhee lived was chosen as the site. Rose Belle, though tiny in population size, was a major sugar estate and had its own factory where Dookhee would send the sugarcane harvested in his plantations to be milled.

It took approximately five years for the first temple to be built on those premises. Bodhini Hoolas, a well-to-do Indian lady, funded Gaurdas' trip to India, where he purchased a Shiva lingam, with Dookhee covering its cost. Sadly, Gaurdas passed away upon his return. A pandit named Ganapatidas, stepped forward, taking the Shiva lingam in his care until it was finally consecrated at the temple in 1911. That it took about a decade for the temple to be built, spoke volume about the social and economic conditions in those days, and yet

Dookhee provided continuous assistance in spite of the challenges.

As progress was slow, perhaps due to the lack of faith from the community or the austerity of the times, those who hoped in completing the temple had no one to turn to other than Dookhee. Pandits Raghooni and Ganapatidas were among these individuals. Pandit Raghooni was an influential person in the southern part of the island and there was a mutual respect between him and Dookhee. Pandit Ganapatidas was one of the few literate persons of the Indo-Mauritian community in those days. He, too, valued Dookhee's involvement with the temple and encouraged him to read the religious scriptures. Gradually, Dookhee came to appreciate the significance of establishing these religious edifices in a community that, for decades, had been deprived of a sound cultural grounding. As the works at the temple resumed, thanks to Dookhee's generosity, a four-foot tall stonewall was erected to secure the premises. A total of five temples were built in the compound, the first of which was to house the deities Shiva and Parvati, whose statues were bought by Dookhee. Other individuals also made contributions and donations, in the form of bells, a water tank, a Nandi (a sacred cow idol) and so forth. The temples were each dedicated to a particular deity and their statues were adorned with golden jewellery offered by Dookhee even though, in those days, the economic situation did not permit the use of gold, and that ornaments worn by women were mostly of copper and silver.

Dookhee had to face a lot of setbacks and criticism while funding the construction and maintenance of the temple. At times, and because of the mistakes of others, the money he donated would be misplaced or misused; yet even then, he never held anybody in contempt nor saw the need to sue anyone. Dookhee was never seen in a court and was against giving grief to people. Instead, his mission was to see to it that the temple and the priest officiating there were being properly looked after. He was always fair to those around him and stepped back from those who cheated him of his money and honesty.

While his time and effort were spent with the temple, called the Narmadeshwar Shivala, Dookhee's other activities also flourished. By 1915, he was a renowned plantation owner, having purchased larger and larger plots of land where sugarcane was cultivated. Now a landlord himself, he treated his workers justly and kindly, and they, in return, held him in high esteem. He knew the pain and struggle they had to endure for he had faced the same hardship. What also mattered to him was that the women on his plantations should also be encouraged to work alongside the men, whether it was to do with weaving baskets, helping with the cattle-rearing, or cultivating crops other than sugarcane. He had witnessed how his mother, and other women in the Deux Bras estate, had to help with the daily tasks in order to bring enough food to their homes.

From their humble home in New Grove, the Gungah family was finally able to afford building large colonial-style houses for them. Dookhee ensured that each one of his seven brothers had their own. They were all identical and in proximity with one another, along the same road in New Grove, signifying the tightknit nature of the family. A quality that was essential for their prosperity. These houses were not typical of the dwellings of the wider Indo-Mauritian community who, in those days, and until much later in the 20th century, lived in small wooden huts. As their name suggests, these colonial houses were much like the ones found on the estates owned by the white descendants of the French who had come to Mauritius in the early 18th century.

The Gungahs' houses had an air of opulence. The wooden-floored rooms were lavishly adorned with exquisite colonial-style furniture, grand French windows would let the fresh

Gungah Family, 1912

countryside air and the delicate light flood the house, large wooden exterior double doors gave on to spacious front and rear verandas that were supported by lush mahogany columns, and black teak shingles glistened on twin sloping roofs. The central courtyard was paved with basalt stones and provided the much-needed space for a busy household. In those days, the kitchen, built mostly of stone, was its own separate yet imposing unit, at the back of the house. The luxurious decoration aside, the cosiness that they provided to the family was testimony of Dookhee's concern for the comfort of his kin. That did not mean that the mansions were all for show and superficiality. Dookhee encouraged everyone, his brothers, their wives and children, to be self-sufficient and provide for their kitchen and larder from their own gardens in their spacious backyards. A larger compound, with fowls and farm animals and a vast orchard were run for the common use of the family and for pleasure. Stables for horses were also on the compound, and stags were free to roam the premises, some of them even venturing into the verandas.

* * * * *

Everything seemed to be set for the Gungahs after fortune had smiled upon them but Fowdur's journey, one that had begun so long ago from the modest village in India, finally came to an end. It is believed that he passed away in 1915 at the age of eighty-five. It was likely that, at that time, Dookhee travelled to India, to his father's native village, perhaps for his last rites, to return his ashes to Ganga. Who knows? But what we know is that, once in Ruwanee, which had not seemed to have changed much ever since Fowdur had bid farewell to it, Dookhee witnessed how deprived the villagers were and had a well dug[7] so they could have access to clean water, at

---

7. Dookhee's contribution carried on for some time with him sending funds for the maintenance of the well and for the benefit of the villagers.

the very least. Among Hindus, the construction of a temple and digging of a well are considered acts of piety. The villagers felt redeemed thanks to Dookhee's generosity.

Four years later, on the 15th of September, Busmoteea passed away at the relatively young age of sixty-seven. She had been a pillar in Dookhee's life and in that of the family. There is no doubt that she had been a role model for her sons for, even though it was predominantly a male household, their respect and support for women shone later in their adulthood. They all encouraged their wives and daughters to partake in the running of the various family duties and responsibilities.

Dookhee had been a pious individual throughout his life – a trait he must have inherited from his parents. Yet, in the early 1900s, Brahmin priests were not officiating at his house whether it was for wedding ceremonies, funerals or other rituals. However, having witnessed the type of devout person that Dookhee was, particularly during the construction of Narmadeshwar Shivala, Pandit Raghooni chose to bring an end to this discrimination and performed all those religious services in a proper manner. In so doing, Pandit Raghooni had brought in a social reform with the help of Dookhee. Gradually, as this practice became more and more accepted in society, thanks to Dookhee's piety and renown, the Brahmins and priests formally recognised this revolution by passing a resolution at the Maha Sabha, an Indo-Mauritian socio-cultural organisation of high authority that was founded in 1925.

The existence of these socio-cultural organisations in the early part of the 20th century was in fact a sign of the fragmentation of the Indo-Mauritian community at the time. There was no real cohesion among the Hindus as each would rally only those who shared their religious philosophy or caste. On the one hand there were the orthodox Hindus and on the other, the liberals. On one stratum, the upper caste and on the other, the lower caste. And finally, the rich and the poor.

Dookhee saw past these immaterial divisions and helped each and every one, whether financially or otherwise. He sought to unify Hindus regardless of their creed, wealth, or aspirations. And he did so without seeking any reward or recognition.

The Narmadeshwar Shivala was not the only temple that Dookhee had helped with even though it was the one that was perhaps most dear to him[8], for he dedicated almost thirty years of his life selflessly to it. Even today, the temple is still run with the help of Dookhee's descendants, the Gungah family. There are too many temples and religious institutions to list but suffices to say that Dookhee gave to all of them whether they were for the Hindi or non-Hindi speaking community, whether it was close to his village in New Grove or anywhere else on the island, whether it was to the orthodox or liberal Hindus. If it weren't through financial help, he would generously donate plots of land and building materials for the construction of these institutions and welfare centres. Whatever was in his means to help the advancement of society, he gave; unconditionally.

Not only did it matter to Dookhee that the community had a place of worship, but he also encouraged everyone to attend these temples. Each year, during the holy festival signifying the Great Night of Shiva, or Maha Shivaratri, where devotees from New Grove and the surrounding villages would go on a pilgrimage[9] to the sacred lake at Grand Bassin in the southern

---

8. More than passively funding the running of the temple, Dookhee took an active role in its management. He was often criticised for his work by those who envied his position and status, but he saw past all of this for his dedication to the temple, the community and Hinduism was of greater importance.

9. The first pilgrimage took place in 1898 with initially only nine devotees, mostly priests, who undertook the journey by foot from a village in the northern part of the island to the lake in Grand Bassin. Pandit Gossagne Nepal had dreamt, the previous year, that there was a sacred lake whose water was as divine and pure as that of the river Ganga. He then proceeded to walk all the way from his village in Terre Rouge in search of the lake which he discovered in Grand Bassin. The following year, him and eight other devotees went on the first pilgrimage.

part of the island to collect the holy water and offer thanks to Lord Shiva, Dookhee ensured that they were all provided with their dhotis, pagris and kanwars[10], all of which he had personally donated. He would also send his workers to help gather the villagers early in the morning and encourage them to go on the pilgrimage. Dookhee also made sure that the pilgrims were given refreshments and a place of rest at the Narmadeshwar Shivala when they had brought back the holy water from the sacred lake to the temple. A two-mile-long queue of pilgrims would gather for the celebrations and prayers. He was adamant that the villagers realised the importance of partaking in these religious ceremonies lest they lost their sense of identity and belonging.

The pilgrimage to Grand Bassin began in 1898 and has taken place ever since. However, from the region surrounding New Grove, a place called Bois Cheri, there was no access to the sacred lake that was on the west side of that village. To resolve this, Dookhee sent his workers to clear a path through the woods and so, in 1920, made possible the opening of the road from Bois Cheri to Grand Bassin for the benefit of the pilgrims. In recognition of Dookhee's contributions to the community, the Governor of Mauritius, Sir Hesketh Bell, visited the Narmadeshwar Shivala in 1921. For such a high dignitary to visit a Hindu temple in those days was a momentous occasion. This was the second largest temple on the island at the time and was at the service of the inhabitants of the southern part of Mauritius.

During another important Hindu festival called Diwali, he would place his gramophone by an open window that gave on to the front veranda and play music so that the neighbouring villagers could rejoice in the entertainment. There was no radio

---

10. A kanwar is a wooden structure, consisting essentially of a pole and containers on either side, whose function is to carry the holy water from the lake back to the temple for the rituals, prayers and offerings to Shiva.

Narmadeshwar Shivala

or television in those days and so a crowd would gather on the roadside to listen to both devotional and popular film songs, and they would stay till dusk so they could admire the decorations and mesmerising illumination from hundreds of diyas (small earthen lamps) beautifully arranged all around the house, on the front steps of the veranda, the handrails and all along the driveway leading from the house to the road. It was a sight to behold in the days when electricity hadn't yet reached the common household.

At Christmas, Dookhee would send generous gifts to the owners and senior management of the sugar factories that milled the sugarcane from his various sugarcane plantations. Children from several orphanages were treated to an annual lunch at his house and they, too, were showered with gifts. Pandits and other scholars of Hinduism were pampered by his charity. And, of course, every member of the large extended Gungah family, comprising at least a hundred individuals, as well as the household staff all received copious gifts on New Year's celebration.

Dookhee's generosity was such that he was compared to the legendary Indian king, Harischandra, in that whoever went to see him for a request never returned empty-handed. These acts of philanthropy were innate to him and did not stop with temples or religious activities, even though these were of crucial importance to the Indo-Mauritian community.

In 1882, there were about a hundred state and aided schools (those receiving subsidies from the government) and were mostly for the minority white and coloured[11] population. The majority of the population, the Indo-Mauritians, did not have access to formal education. By 1908, little had changed whereas Dookhee personally ran dozens of schools, in different parts of the island. He financed every single aspect of these schools, from all running costs to maintenance, to supplying thousands of books freely to students, paying for the teachers' salaries, awarding prizes, clothes and small items of jewellery (particularly for the girls) to the deserving students, and issuing certificates.

Sending children to school was not as straightforward as it might seem. Even when the government schools were opened across the island, rumour was spreading that the educational system would convert all students to Christianity and so the Indo-Mauritians were reluctant to send their children to school. Beside a few baitkas, there was an acute lack of access to education in general, not just religious studies. Dookhee realised how detrimental this was to the children of the Indo-Mauritian community and therefore opened a number of schools and worked with an Indian scholar, named Atmaram Vishwanath, to come up with a proper curriculum. In the 1920s, Dookhee's schools were the first in the country to have a

---

11. Those of mixed white and non-white heritage.

syllabus to teach various subjects, including mathematics, history and geography, in a Hindi medium – a language the vast majority of the Indo-Mauritians were comfortable with. The syllabus was circulated in all schools as a booklet. In addition, textbooks devised by Vishwanath and financed by Dookhee were freely distributed to every single student. These were known as the *Dookhee Gungah Hindi Reading* books. Dookhee provided teachers with financial incentives to encourage them to bring more children to his schools. He even had inspectors visit the schools to ensure the proper running of these institutions.

Kunwar Maharaj Singh was an Indian government delegate sent to Mauritius to inquire into the state of the Indian immigrants. From 19th of December 1924 to 31st of January 1925, Maharaj Singh carried out his investigation. He visited sugar plantations and estates and met with several dignitaries as well as planters and labourers. On the 11th of January, he was a guest at the Narmadeshwar Shivala where, at the back of the compound, one of Dookhee's schools had been established. There, Maharaj Singh praised Dookhee's numerous achievements and his promotion of free education. In his report published in 1925, Maharaj Singh recommended that Indian languages should be taught at school, a comment that was no doubt inspired by Dookhee's Hindi-medium schools.

Some months later, Dookhee was addressed a letter dated 7th of September 1925 from Natal (now Durban) praising his good deeds in the field of education and requesting more copies of his *Dookhee Gungah Hindi Reading* books as they were the only Hindi textbooks they could easily get hold of. This level of recognition for a descendant of an indentured labourer was unheard of in those days. His influence on the lives of several hundreds, if not thousands, of children was monumental and he was truly a pioneer of free education for the masses.

Scholars of Hinduism and pandits at Dookhee Gungah's residence, 1934

It was a lifelong commitment to education for Dookhee. In 1930, he set up the Savitri Girls School[12] to further reform women's position in society. Dookhee had always been about the emancipation and empowerment of the womenfolk by providing them access to paid work on his estates, his biscuit factories, bakeries, cattle farms, fisheries and cottage industry. With the Savitri Girls School he wanted to make sure that girls would have an even stronger foundation in education and access to better opportunities compared to the previous generation.

Even though there had been some progress in the living conditions and lifestyle among the Indo-Mauritian community since they first arrived en masse in 1834, in the early 1900s there was what could be described as a cultural atrophy. Dookhee, once again the visionary, was already organising satsangs, or gatherings where religious discourses were held by scholars of Hinduism, whether at the Narmadeshwar Shivala or other temples or even at his own house. His incalculable wealth did not make him pompous in any way. Instead, he made several important contributions to religious and cultural societies with the aim to incentivise the community to be more engaged in their cultural and social duties. These organisations gradually realised that there was indeed a demand for these types of social activities. As a result, the 1920s were marked by the visits of several cultural leaders from India. They had been invited by these organisations to help consolidate the work that had already begun by Dookhee and other stalwarts in the community. These leaders toured the island and popularised the use of Hindi among the Indo-Mauritians. The most outstanding of these leaders was Ramgovind Trivedi, a journalist and scholar of Indian philosophy

---

12. Savitribai Phule (1831-1897) was perhaps the first woman teacher of modern India. Savitribai and her husband founded one of the early modern Indian girls' schools in Pune in 1851. The Savitri Girls School was likely named after the pioneer of India's feminist movement.

who had translated the *Rig Vedas* from Sanskrit into Hindi. With Dookhee's help, he opened a dozen centres across the island for the study of the *Bhagavad Gita*. Upon his return to India, Trivedi published a magazine and named it *"Gungah"* in honour of Dookhee. The magazine was issued every quarter between 1927 and 1933 in Vanarasi. Another publication that is of huge historical importance was the first ever Hindi book to be published in Mauritius by Vishwanath, called *History of Mauritius*[13].

13. More on this book in Part Two.

Legacy – 1930s Onward

As the 1930s began, Mauritius came out of the Great Depression that had started from about 1922. Most planters and sugar estate owners suffered through this crisis, but not Dookhee. His acumen and entrepreneurship would allow him to not only navigate through these hard times but to prosper while carrying on with his philanthropy. He did not have to preach about his social work and charity – his deeds carried more weight than the value of his donations. He had many admirers, both among his workers and the public. His workers were in awe of him, and he inspired them to work hard like he had. From time to time, Dookhee was called upon to mediate between disputing parties. He did so in all fairness and judiciously, and his ruling was final. Such was his reputation.

Dookhee's success relied a lot on the support of his wife, Mooneea, and his family, particularly his brothers. Each one of them was responsible for one of the various activities that Dookhee was involved in. One brother looked after all the religious aspects and even managed some of the socio-cultural organisations. Another was responsible for the schools and educational elements, yet another took care of the estates and various properties. The youngest oversaw the bakery, and the rest were each in charge of the several other cottages, orchards, fisheries, farms, etc. There was a lot to handle as a business for the family. *La Société Dookhee Gungah et Compagnie* was founded in 1930 by Dookhee and five of his brothers specifically for that purpose. Dookhee, as the head of the family, also oversaw the entire family enterprise, very much like the CEO of a conglomerate. Over the decades, to manage seven sugar estates was no mean feat. It is estimated that the total land that he owned at one point was the equivalent of about ten times the total area of Hyde Park or about forty times the size of the Botanical Garden in Pamplemousses. Much of the estates has either been donated unreservedly to several institutions and the government by Dookhee for the betterment of the community and nation, or passed down the generations among the ever-growing number of heirs. Part of his orchard was given to the government so that the airport could be extended during the Second World War, and the remaining portion is now managed by the government and used as an agricultural experimentation station. The orchard now bears the name of *Dookhee Gungah Orchard.*

Within the confines of his house in New Grove, there were several gatherings whereby Dookhee and his guests, whom he picked judiciously, debated the current state of affairs and talked about setting up a structure for socio-cultural and even political organisations. In particular, the wealthy estate owners would convene at Dookhee's house and had lengthy conversations about the sugar boom and bust of the 1920s and 1930s, respectively. Similarly, those who fought to bring a political voice to the Indo-Mauritian community would seek Dookhee's wisdom in proposing the first Indo-Mauritians candidacy to the general elections in the 1920s and, subsequently, oversee the election of Dunputh Lallah and Rajcoomar Gujadhur as members of the Legislative Council. In parallel, the rise of the working-class activists such as Maurice Curé and Guy Rozemont were topical exchanges among Dookhee and his erudite guests. His views were highly regarded among his peers, and the support he provided to emerging political figures such as the Bissoondoyal brothers and Sir Seewoosagur Ramgoolam, who would eventually become the country's first Prime Minister when Mauritius gained independence from the British in 1968, were crucial in determining the future of the country.

Dookhee's house, to some extent, had been the crucible where many of these socio-political movements took shape and later burst into the political scene of a nascent nation. He might not have taken an active role in politics himself in the riper years of his life but his influence and impact on the destiny of the country was undeniably fundamental.

One other topic that was also addressed during those meetings was the centenary celebration of the arrival of Indian indentured labourers in 1935. In commemoration of this historic event, Dookhee published a book called *Sadukti Sangraha*. It was a collection of inspirational sayings derived from religious scriptures, and it was a testimony that Dookhee was well versed in both Hindi and Sanskrit. He had taught himself to read and write after having spent years in the company of learned pandits and scholars while encouraging them, in return, to disseminate the teachings from the *Bhagavad Gita*, *Ramayana* and *Vedas* to a culturally thirsty Indo-Mauritian community. His book stands among those works that hold a historically significant place. To commemorate the centenary of the arrival of Indian immigrants with a book about their cultural and religious identity is a metaphor about how vital this sense of a common faith was to the survival and emancipation of the indentured labourers.

On 23rd of November 1978, the then Governor General, Dayendranath Burrenchobay, inaugurated the Dookhee Gungah Government School near New Grove in recognition of his immeasurable contribution to the field of education. The school was built on a plot of land that once belonged to Dookhee. Several dignitaries were present at the ceremony, and they

Gungah Family, 1931

all recognised the work of this unique individual who had never set foot in a classroom and who had never been formally taught to read and write. The dozens of schools that were once under his ownership and management no longer exist but the countless children who benefited from them at no cost are the true legacy of his contribution to educating a nation.

* * * * *

Dookhee Gungah's story is one of unparalleled achievement and positive impact on society. While most stories about indentureship revolve around suffering and hardship (and understandably so), his is about the rise of not just one individual or family but that of an entire nation, for he was the first to inspire, support and guide the leaders who came after him.

He provided the oppressed Indo-Mauritian community with the means to better themselves, to find their new sense of identity, to be able to freely practice their religion, to have access to free education, to learn about their culture and traditions, and to unite as one people.

Dookhee has been described by many of his contemporaries as a benefactor, philanthropist, social reformer, promoter of knowledge, father of free education, author, entrepreneur, patron of arts and culture, administrator, landlord, commander and immortal fighter of Hinduism, amongst other accolades. These take on a different, more pointed meaning when one considers the context in which these praises were bestowed. The challenges and hurdles the Indo-Mauritian community had to face, even though they were more populous than the ruling class, were truly set for them not to succeed. To be fair, few did manage to rise and serve their community, but none did it to the extent that Dookhee did. While others had to rally together to fight one cause, he independently, and out of his own pocket, championed several of them.

Cover of Dookhee's book, *Sadukti Sangraha*

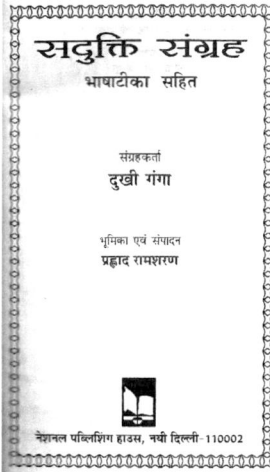

Title page of the book

दुखी गंगा
(1867–1944)

दुखी गंगा का जन्म 11 अगस्त, 1867 को दे ब्रा शक्कर कोठी कैंप में हुआ था। इनके पिता गिरमिट मज़दूर के रूप में 1854 को रावनी ग्राम, चौरसिया परगना, आरा ज़िले से मॉरिशस गये थे। दुखी गंगा आठ भाइयों में अग्रज थे। अपनी यौवनावस्था से कड़ी मेहनत करके, वे मज़दूर से एक प्रतिष्ठित ज़मींदार के रूप में उभरे। ये स्वभाव से धार्मिक थे और विद्वानों के संसर्ग में रहते थे। सन् 1900 के बाद इन्होंने रोसबेल के नर्मदेश्वर मंदिर के निर्माण तथा उसके रख-रखाव में भारी योगदान दिया।

इन्होंने अपने ख़र्च पर हिंदी और संस्कृत की अनेक पाठशालाएं खुलवायीं। पंडित आत्माराम विश्वनाथ से बाल पुस्तक मालाओं का निर्माण करवाया। पं. राममनोहर शर्मा से हिंदी पाठ्यक्रम तैयार करवाया। 'मॉरिशस का इतिहास' जैसे ग्रंथ के प्रकाशन के लिए लेखक को आर्थिक सहायता दी। सन् 1935 में इन्होंने 'सदुक्ति संग्रह' पुस्तक का संकलन भी किया। देश में अनेक धार्मिक एवं सांस्कृतिक संस्थाओं के निर्माण में इन्होंने भारी योगदान दिया। दुखी गंगा मॉरिशस के भारतवंशियों में एक अविस्मरणीय सांस्कृतिक नेता के रूप में प्रसिद्ध हुए। इनका देहांत 24 मार्च, 1944 को हुआ।

Inside cover of *Sadukti Sangraha* containing a short note about Dookhee

And while many had to rely on the government and other organisations to provide them with their basic needs, he single-handedly operated as an institution who empowered women and supported their emancipation, who provided free access to education for those seeking a better life, who supported other socio-cultural entities so they could in turn shepherd the community through their hardship, who ran businesses and enabled hundreds of families to earn a decent livelihood, who managed vast estates that contributed to the economy of a prospering nation, and so on and so forth. And he did it all out of pure philanthropy, with no expectation of fame or recompense.

His assets and property spanned across more than just real estate, like that of most planters. He owned a bakery, fishery, biscuit factory, farm, orchard, an entire cottage industry, several colonial-style houses, bungalows by the seaside and countryside, boats, cars, lorries, horses and carriages, locomotives, weighbridges and other possessions and items of luxury that were rare or unheard of among the Indo-Mauritian community. His real worth, however, was in the construction of several temples, the funding of religious ceremonies and festivals, schools, textbooks, financing of political activists, and helping his fellow Mauritians rise as a nation.

He and his family might have lived affluently and in abundance, but it was never out of greed or avarice. In fact, his benevolence was legendary and revered, and unequalled. Vishwanath said of Dookhee, "His generosity is more valuable to us than his wealth." It was hard for some to understand Dookhee's ascent and prosperity. Legend has it that, once upon a time, while toiling in the sugarcane field, Fowdur had stumbled upon a dazzling treasure – not unlike the gold the indentured labourers were promised to find if they were to dig underneath the boulders in the plantations. This treasure was to be the source of the Gungahs' extraordinary fortune, according to folklore. But these were mere fabrications by those

Raghubur Gungah with his wife (L), and son Khemraj (R), 1942

who envied Dookhee's fame. None of this was to put a dent in his dedication to social work and charity. He symbolised the true meaning of philanthropy – the absolute unconditional love of humanity.

His legacy is still alive and, even though it cannot be quantified, his contribution to society is of immense historical importance. He was recognised in his native Mauritius, his father's native India, as well as in South Africa. For a son of an immigrant to have that much reach during the period of indentured servitude is perhaps unique among the entire indentureship diaspora[14].

A heartfelt obituary was published in a renowned weekly newspaper, called *Arya Vir*, on the 31st of March 1944. He was 76 when he passed away a week before, on the 24th. His grave can be found on the cremation ground that was once

---

14. The diaspora consists mainly of Indians who were dispatched to the following colonies: Mauritius, Seychelles, Réunion, South and East Africa, the Caribbean, Suriname, Guyana, Malaysia and Singapore.

used by the family and is in the vicinity of New Grove. Mauritius has undoubtedly gained from the life of a true visionary, pioneer and philanthropist.

The following engraving, which encapsulates the person that he was, can be seen on Dookhee Gungah's headstone:

How fortunate is the man
Whose life is spent in the spread of knowledge,
And whose path is that of virtue,
Whose conduct is free from selfishness and pride,
And whose sole aim is benevolence
For the happiness of suffering mankind

PART TWO

A Book Like No Other

A Brief History

A century ago, in 1923, the first Hindi book ever written in Mauritius was awaiting to be published. It was about the history of the island and aptly titled *Mauritius Ka Itihas* (*History of Mauritius* in Hindi). Its author was Pandit Atmaram Vishwanath, an Indian journalist and scholar.

There are a few questions that surround this book. For example, what is its historical significance? Who was its author and what was his motivation to publish such a book? And, interestingly, why did its eventual publication spark uproar among a group of Indo-Mauritians? The answers to these questions have ultimately led me to find out more about the person to whom the book was dedicated. For he is not just a mention in a book – he is someone whose life has many chapters, each one more extraordinary than the other. His own story is still relevant, even a hundred years later, but we won't dwell on it for now.

To appreciate the importance of *History of Mauritius*, we first have to understand the historical context of that period. In the early 1900s, Mauritius was under the British rule. The majority of the population was ethnically of Indian origin, but it was neither a homogenous nor a cohesive Indo-Mauritian community as there was little to keep them unified. Some Hindus would try to rally the community together, but they were each looking out for those who shared their religious philosophy or caste. There were the orthodox Hindus on one side and the liberals on the other. Besides, the upper caste was unlikely to mingle with the lower caste. The wealthier among them would not necessarily interact with those less fortunate. The one thing which could unite the Hindus was their common language, Hindi, and other aspects of their culture such as the arts and religious discourses. Unfortunately, there was limited access to Hindi literature in general as most publications available then were either in French or English, given the colonial past of Mauritius. The Indo-Mauritians, thus, lacked something or someone that could bring them together and inspire them to delve deeper into their cultural heritage.

A local newspaper, called *The Hindustani*, was the first and only one, among a dozen French and English papers that existed then, that was accessible to the Hindu community for it was printed mostly in Hindi and partly in English. The weekly paper was originally launched in 1909 and edited by Manilal Doctor, an Indian barrister and linguist. He had come to Mauritius a couple of years earlier on 11th October 1907 upon the request of Mahatma Gandhi, who had advised him to help the Indo-Mauritians labourers in their plight to improve their social and political situation. He did so fervently until his departure in 1911.

In 1912, Pandit Atmaram Vishwanath came to Mauritius from India, upon the insistence of Manilal Doctor, to take over the running of *The Hindustani*, which he edited for about a year until the newspaper ceased to be published. Even then, Vishwanath chose to stay in Mauritius, having witnessed the conditions in which the Indo-Mauritians were living. He followed in Manilal Doctor's footstep in helping to uplift the Hindu community through social work. During that time, he spent about seven years researching and compiling his seminal book, *History of Mauritius,* which he finally wrote in 1921.

The work that went into the book was indeed colossal. Beside the main historical events of Mauritius, outlining its Portuguese, Dutch, French and British occupation, the book also looked into other subjects such as the indentured servitude system and the treatment of Indian workers in Mauritius, their religious, cultural and educational conditions, key political figures, and the democratic system of government in the island. The challenge for the author was that he did not have readily available references, whether in Hindi or English, as most books then were in French. One of the very few English history books available at the time was called *Mauritius (Illustrated)* by Allister MacMillan, a voluminous book on various historical, commercial and descriptive elements of Mauritius. It was printed in London in 1914 following MacMillan's exploratory visit to the British colony. It is likely that Vishwanath had read MacMillan's book as part of his own research for there are sections in *History of Mauritius* that are inspired from it.

In any case, *History of Mauritius* is a book like no other. It was a first of its kind and, following its subsequent publication in 1923, inspired other emerging Indo-Mauritian scholars to write their own books about various aspects of Mauritian history and culture. It was not to be as straightforward as this, however. The publication of the book itself was delayed for about two years. One of the reasons was the lack of funding for its printing and so Vishwanath had to seek sponsorship from a handful of wealthy Indo-Mauritian dignitaries. In addition, as soon as the book was released in Mauritius, in late July 1923, it caused a stir, particularly among the high-echelon society of Indo-Mauritians. The reasons for this are twofold.

First, they accused Vishwanath of being a liar and a fraud for having misrepresented the Indian community in Mauritius. They threatened to burn copies of the book and have the author deported back to India. This whole scene took place on 7th August 1923 in Port Louis, the capital of Mauritius, where Vishwanath was being manhandled and insulted by this group of individuals. The embarrassing incident was reported on that

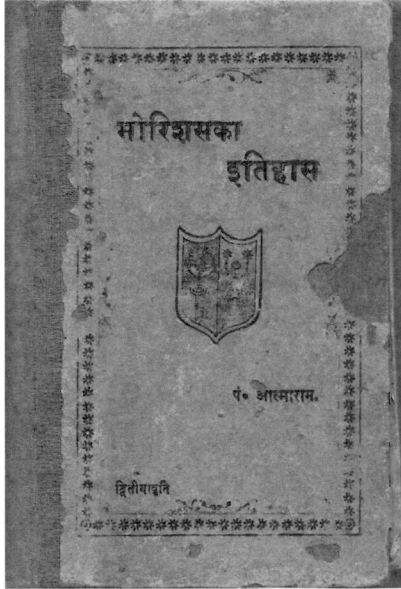

Cover of the first edition of History of Mauritius, 1923

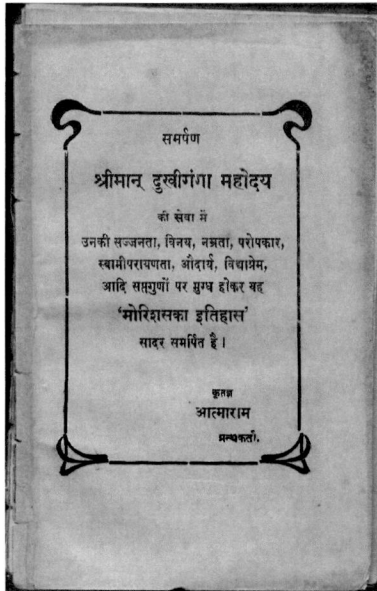

Page from the first edition of History of Mauritius, 1923, showing the book to be dedicated to Dookhee Gungah

Pandit Vishwanath is assaulted in Port Louis following the publication of his book

day in the oldest and one of the most popular newspapers of the time, *Le Cernéen*, in an article entitled *Un Verte Correction* (*A Severe Reprimand*, in French).

Second, they were not happy that the book had been dedicated to a non-Brahmin Hindu. It angered them that such a person should be the recipient of that much praise and recognition. The person in question was Dookhee Gungah, a renowned social worker and entrepreneur. Why, then, this protest against Gungah? This speaks volume about the prevailing attitude, at that time, towards those of a different caste.

The criticisms and threats ensued for a number of weeks after the book's release. Fortunately, once the misunderstandings had been dissipated and the author having come forward to justify why he had dedicated the book to Gungah, the dispute was laid to rest. Following a few edits to the original book, more so to please certain sections of the Indo-Mauritian community, the author published the second edition of *History of Mauritius* in April 1924, again with the financial help of a few individuals including that of Gungah. Moreover, Vishwanath insisted that despite some changes in the second edition he would keep the original acknowledgement to Dookhee Gungah as he considered this to be of utmost importance to the *raison d'être* of the book. As he explains in the acknowledgement, the book would not have been published in the first place without the constant encouragement and financial support from Gungah. He titled the acknowledgement "Brahman's Benediction", meaning that he wanted to bestow that highest form of recognition and gratitude, i.e., the blessing of Brahma, the Hindu god associated with creation and knowledge.

Who, therefore, was Dookhee Gungah? An entire book could be written about his achievements alone. He was the eldest son of Indian indentured labourers. His father came to Mauritius on 27th September 1854 and his mother on 18th July 1857. He was born on 11th August 1867, amid an outbreak of malaria and other natural calamities, and grew up in deplorable conditions and abject poverty. Despite this, he rose to become the epitome of social work and benevolence towards his fellow compatriots. In many ways, from the early 1880s till late 1930s, he was a pioneer and leader in various social and cultural fields. Such was his impact on society that he had been qualified by his contemporaries as, among other notable things, a social reformer, patron of the arts and culture, pioneer of free education, promoter of knowledge, champion of Mauritian historicity, author, benefactor, entrepreneur, administrator, etc. Although he might not be remembered today as any of these things, his legacy lives on. He embodied the true meaning of philanthropy, the compassion and love for humanity.

The collaboration between Gungah and Pandit Vishwanath did not end with the publication of *History of Mauritius*. In fact, Gungah appointed Vishwanath as inspector to supervise his schools. In the early 1900s, the majority of Indo-Mauritians did not have access to formal education, yet Dookhee Gungah personally financed every aspect of the running of more than a dozen schools in various parts of the country for the benefit of the community. He supplied freely to all his students thousands of textbooks, which himself and Vishwanath had devised. He also paid for the teachers' and inspectors' salaries, provided financial incentives to teachers who encourage children to attend his schools, he awarded various prizes and certificates to the best deserving students, and so on. The Hindi textbooks that were written by Vishwanath in the mid-1920s were the most sought-after textbooks for decades. On 7th September 1925, Gungah was addressed a letter from Durban, South Africa, praising his good deeds in the field of education and requesting more copies of the *Dookhee Gungah Hindi Series* textbooks that Pandit Vishwanath had written.

Dookhee Gungah went on to finance almost all of Pandit Vishwanath's books, but none of them had the same impact that *History of Mauritius* had when it was first released. To mark its 75th anniversary of publication in 1998, Dookhee Gungah's grandson, Dr Kooshalanund Gungah, partially sponsored the third edition of the book, which was re-edited by the eminent Mauritian historian and scholar, Pahlad Ramsurrun. More recently, in 2012, Ramsurrun edited the English translation of *Mauritius Ka Itihas*, which made the book even more accessible to the wider public. This book should be a reference for everyone, not only for its content but mostly for its great historical value.

The English translation of Pandit Atmaram Vishwanath's acknowledgment to Dookhee Gungah:

Brahman's Benediction

The name of Dookhee Gungah is well-known all over Mauritius. Young and old, everyone knows him. His past is like that of so many of his contemporaries whose parents were brought to Mauritius as contractual labourers under the indentured servitude system. Dookhee's father came from the province of Bihar, in India, and worked through hardships and suffered for many years, living in abject poverty. Dookhee is his eldest son whom he begot while living in those destitute conditions. As a reminder of his humble beginnings, he gave his son the befitting name *"Dookhee"*, meaning *Unfortunate.* However, through his benevolence and good deeds towards others, Dookhee made of himself a person of good fortune.

I do not wish to count how much he has in his bank account, the number of horses, carriages, servants, homes, cars and acres of land that he possesses. If I do recount all of these, I could write an entire book on this subject. There are several other rich and prosperous Indo-Mauritians like him, and perhaps even richer. That he is a millionaire is undeniable and he has earned every cent through his sheer hard work. But I have not set my eyes on his wealth. More than that, I admire his charity and liberal heart, and this is what my eyes will rest upon. His generosity is more valuable to us than his wealth.

He is always happy to help unreservedly and without hesitation anyone, be they strangers, Brahmins, beggars, the poor and helpless, orphans, hermits, pariahs, saints, paupers, pilgrims, or someone from a social or religious organisation seeking a donation. The *Narmadeshwar Shivala* of Rose-Belle is a concrete example of his generosity. He has set up a school there for students to be taught in their mother tongue. He personally bears all its running costs. What other act of piety is higher or nobler than the dissemination of knowledge? Others, particularly the rich, should take note of this.

We hear of the legend of Raja Harishchandra, from the Puranas (the Hindu epics), who was famous for his charity. We can say with certitude that no one who goes to Shri Dookhee Gungah with a request returns empty-handed. He fulfils the wishes of everyone and, on rare occasions perhaps, meets those needs at least in parts.

He did not have the opportunity to attend school for any formal education but his sense of decency, his civility, gentlemanliness, politeness, humility, generosity, eloquence and his peaceful character is more significant than that of any other educated person. He ranks among saints and sages as far as selflessness, sense of religiosity and philanthropy are concerned.

Shri Dookhee Gungah is a person of excellence and distinguished qualities. His home is a model of an extended Hindu family. He has five brothers, and they live happily with all their family members. There is peace and happiness in their homes.

I have stated earlier that Shri Dookhee Gungah is a promoter of knowledge and contributes substantially for education. Writing or helping to write something is also a significant part of the activities pertaining to education. His encouragement and financial assistance have contributed to this book, "*History of Mauritius*".

I am indebted to Dookhee Gungah for this holy and invaluable work. I spend day and night wondering how to redeem this debt. I do not have anything of value to give him apart from my heartfelt gratitude. I wholeheartedly pray to the Almighty that Shri Dookhee Gungah carries on serving the people and, in return, that he prospers, and grant him everlasting respect, health and long life for the sake of the Mauritian community. May he be blessed with many children and grandchildren and remain forever an example to Indo-Mauritians and others. I hope that my readers will join me in this prayer to bestow our blessings upon him.

Politely Yours,
Pandit Atmaram Vishwanath
Author of *History of Mauritius*, 1923

End Note

Dookhee Gungah's story is one whose time has come. His story touches on so many aspects that are now more relevant than ever. Whether it is to do with philanthropy, in its most fundamental and purest form[15], or whether it is about empowerment or entrepreneurship or emancipation, everything that Dookhee did was in one way or another a ground-breaking and laudable achievement. He was a pioneer in Mauritius and, perhaps, even among the diaspora of indentured labourers and their descendants.

I am eternally indebted towards my father, Dr Kooshalanund Gungah, who has been monumental in reviving my ancestor's story. Without his guidance and encouragement, I would not have been able to produce this work. I am simply adding my own small contribution to the enormous work that my father has already accomplished. He has personally financed the re-edition of both Pandit Vishwanath's book and Dookhee Gungah's book. He has contributed unconditionally to the preservation of the legacy, whether at the Narmadeshwar Shivala, the primary school, or even the orchard named after Dookhee Gungah. There are several other examples where he has fought to have our ancestor's name recognised by historians who, through no fault of their own, were not aware of the magnitude of Dookhee's achievements. This book is therefore

---

15. As opposed to philanthropic activities that are extrinsically a means of tax avoidance, or an opportunity to invest in seemingly lofty ventures that are purely for personal gain, or simply as a trendy thing to do.

a token of my admiration of my father's unwavering dedication to the memory of another great personality. Equally, this book is a gift to the entire Gungah family.

Still, there is much, much more that needs to be told about the life of Dookhee Gungah. This abridged version is only to provide a glimpse of his many achievements and timeless qualities. There was no need to repeat what had already been published about him but the aim was to bring his story to a new audience.

History will remember him as a great philanthropist whose legacy will shine on like an eternal flame. But to me he was much more than that. Philanthropy was his way of being. It wasn't something he would do simply because he was successful. And did more than be charitable and benevolent, although these are laudable qualities in and of themselves. I don't think it's an exaggeration to say that he helped build the crucible from which emerged the champions of Mauritius's development and prosperity. The great leaders and defenders of democracy who came after him have walked the path he helped pave with his vision and devotion. His greatness was far-reaching and will permeate far, far in the future. To remember him is to honour his work and his benevolence.

In 1939, on the occasion of Mahatma Gandhi's seventieth birthday party commemoration, Albert Einstein said in his speech, "Generations to come, it may well be, will scarce believe that such a man as this one ever in flesh and blood walked upon this Earth." Dookhee was a contemporary of the Mahatma and I strongly believe that this quote could very well have applied to him, too. But that's just my view.

Dookhee Gungah will forever be my hero and inspiration.

P.S. The photographs are from the family collection. The illustrations are by my wife, my anchor, Ouma.

Dookhee Gungah, 1920s